HOW TO READ

PEOPLE'S

MIND

Simple Tricks To Study People Through Behavior, Mindset, Predicting Their Emotions, Decision Making.

Benjooba lugard

HOW TO READ PEOPLE'S MIND

BOOK DESCRIPTION

INTRODUCTION

HOW TO READ PEOPLE'S MIND
UNDERSTANDING HUMAN BEHAVIOUR
MORALS AND MINDSET: How REMEMBERING OUR PAST ACTION DRIVES OUR FUTURE BEHAVIOR.
PERSONAL VALUE
PREDICTING PEOPLE EMOTION

CHAPTER ONE

HOW TO READ PEOPLE'S MIND
TRICKS TO STUDY PEOPLE 1
HAVE AN OPEN MIND AND BE IMPARTIAL.
PAY ATTENTION TO APPEARANCE
TRICKS TO STUDY PEOPLE 2
PAY ATTENTION TO PEOPLE POSTURE

CHAPTER TWO

TRICK TO STUDY PEOPLE 3
WATCH THEIR PHYSICAL MOVEMENT
TRICK TO STUDY PEOPLE 4
TRY TO INTERPRETE FACIAL EXPRESSION
TRICKS TO STUDY PEOPLE 5
DON'T RUN AWAY FROM TALK

CHAPTER THREE

Book Description

Book Overview

In this "How To Get People's Mind's"

Learning how to deal with different personalities and type of people and we sharpen our emotional intelligence

Learning how to read the mind of people effectively, the goal is to help you create huge connections with the people around you.

You will learn techniques on deciphering common body language and also learn how the eyes can give you a perspective of non verbal communication.

The goals is to profound influence on the way to think and getting exactly what you want from them.

Everything that you want is connected to developing fulfilling, positive and rewarding relationships with people.

You will also discover how to conduct a behavioral analysis and also common patterns of interpreting behavior.

Some people seem to acquire everything they ask for and how others are most attracted to them?

Understand how your colleagues seems to know what your manager thinks and what is the best thing to say.

INTRODUCTION

When it comes to examining people, it's important to consider a variety of factors. The goal is to start by observing their behavior and body language, as this can

provide valuable insights into their personality and mood. It's important to ask questions and actively listen to their responses, as this can help you understand

People thoughts, feelings, and motivations. Paying attention to people interests, values, and communication styles can help you tailor your interactions to connect. .Ultimately, taking a holistic approach to examining people can help you build

stronger relationships and navigate social situations more easily.

Leaving a good impression is crucial when it comes to presenting yourself well, especially during the initial stages of any relationship. In case you have a rough start, you may still be able to change someone's

perception with time and patience. However, if you can prevent any misunderstandings from the beginning, you

could potentially open up opportunities that you might otherwise miss.For instance, when writing a letter of interest to a company you aspire to work for, it is essential to

Mention your personality traits and skills that align with their organizational values. Failing to do so may lead to your application being overlooked. By highlighting these areas, you can get a head start in the application process.

It's important to know the principle and to get some psychological tricks about understanding human behavior, moral and mindset, predicting people emotions, decision making process

HOW TO READ PEOPLE'S MIND

UNDERSTANDING HUMAN BEHAVIOUR

The study of how and why individuals act and respond in particular ways is known as understanding human behavior. It involves examining the influences and

factors such as heredity, upbringing, culture, and how environment shape human behavior. Understanding

Human behavior can assist towards improving the communication skills, forming stronger

connection and enhancing our overall well-being by providing insights into emotions, decision-making, relationships, and social interactions.

MORALS AND MINDSET: How remembering our past action drives our future behavior.

Some people maintain their moral identity, being completely immoral and being a saintly person. Remembering our good deeds can give us a boost of

energy and make us feel like we have temporarily achieved moral sainthood. This extra moral energy

Allow us to act selflessly and a little more selfishly. if we regard ourselves as moral people. On the other hand, when we think about our

Bad behavior, we tend to feel a moral deficit and try to make up for it by doing good deeds and adding points to our moral goodness. Our activity might be good or

harmful, it is not always necessary for it to be explicitly stated. What matters is that you act in a way that has a

significant impact on moral frameworks. The morality of an action is

determined by the results it produces. The aim of any activity should be, to maximize happiness for greatest number of individuals, while also taking into account of people well-being is important to treat others with respect and to follow moral laws and norms of behavior because of our sense of ethical obligation.

People with lower extraversion had faces where the region around the nose appeared to push against the face, while higher levels of extraversion were linked to more projecting lips and nose. This

suggests that psychological traits may be detectable in a person's face, but additional research is needed to fully understand this phenomenon.

PERSONAL VALUE

Whether you acknowledge them or not, values exist. When you create goals and decisions that are in line with your principles, life would be simple for you. Will you experience internal conflict and

stress? If your job requires you to perform 70-hour work weeks but you love your family? You would

be happy in your career, if you don't enjoy competition

and you work in a highly competitive way satisfy your want .

Knowing your values may be quite helpful in these kinds of circumstances. Knowing your personal values allows you to respond to questions such as these and use them as a guide for making decisions about how to spend your life:

• What career path should I take?

• Do I accept this promotion or not?

• Should I launch a company of my own?

• Do I have to give in or stick to my business?

HOW TO READ PEOPLE'S MIND

Thus, by taking your time to comprehend what the real priorities are in life, you will eventually be able

to decide what course is greatest for you and your objectives!

What would you say your values are?

It's necessary for you to understand what values generally.

The things that you consider significant in your life and career are your values. They establish your priorities and, in secret place, they're probably the yardsticks you use to assess, if your life is going in the direction you'd like it to.

Life is generally wonderful and you are happy when your actions and behavior are consistent with your ideas. However, things feel off, when these don't line up with your personal goals. This may be the cause of your discontent.

PREDICTING PEOPLE EMOTION

Remember that emotions, not reason, are often what motivate individuals. People act on their gut feelings; believe things because it seems to be real,

HOW TO READ PEOPLE'S MIND

and make emotional decisions—even when they claim their justifications are rational. •

You could hear others offering justifications for their actions or words. Occasionally, the justification may seem quite weak. Consider the possibility that the individual doesn't work according to their desire rather than accepting their justification.

•Don't concentrate on rational arguments while trying to convince someone, .Concentrate on leaving an emotional impression. If someone claims to be driven only by reason, it's possible that they lack

Wisdom and they are not unaware of the influence of their emotions.

CHAPTER ONE

HOW TO READ PEOPLE'S MIND

TRICKS TO STUDY PEOPLE 1

HAVE AN OPEN MIND AND BE IMPARTIAL.

You have to practice being open-minded before trying to read others. Keep your feelings and experiences from skewing your perceptions and beliefs.

You will misinterpret individuals, if you are quick to judge them. Approach every contact and circumstance with objectivity.

It's true what I say: "Logic won't tell you the whole story about anybody." To learn how to understand the crucial non-verbal signs that people give out, you have to give up on other essential sources of information.

"Remain objective and receive information neutrally without distorting it" This is what it means to perceive someone clearly.

PAY ATTENTION TO APPEARANCE

Success and ambition Or perhaps their casual attire of jeans and a t-shirt indicates comfort? Are there any pendants that they own that represent their spiritual principles, such a crucifix or a Buddha? You can tell something by what they're wearing, anyhow. All that is required of you is that you pay attention to "identity claims." These are the items that people choose to

display via their looks, including rings, tattoos, or t-shirts with messages.

Consider people's appearances when reading them. What attire are they wearing? Does their clothing convey an air of success and ambition, or do their casual attire of jeans and a t-shirt indicate comfort? Do they wear any pendants that represent their spiritual principles, such as a crucifix or a Buddha? You can tell something by what they're wearing, after all. All that is required of you is that you pay "Identity claims." These are the items that people choose to display through their appearance, including rings, tattoos, or t-shirts with messages.

Identity claims are deliberate declarations about our beliefs, values, aspirations, and attitudes. They are intentional and essential to remember. Some may perceive them as deceptive or manipulative. In my view, most people truly want to be acknowledged and are willing to compromise their appearance. Given the

HOW TO READ PEOPLE'S MIND

Choice, they prefer to be seen as authentic rather than favorable.

TRICKS TO STUDY PEOPLE 2

PAY ATTENTION TO PEOPLE POSTURE

An individual's posture may reveal a lot about their mindset. They are confident when they carry their heads high.

It could be an indication of poor self-esteem if they crouch or stroll indecisively.

Check how they stand to see when they move with confidence, holding their head high, or if they walk unsure or shy away, which are signs of low self-esteem.

HOW TO READ PEOPLE'S MIND

CHAPTER TWO

TRICK TO STUDY PEOPLE 3

WATCH THEIR PHYSICAL MOVEMENT

People communicate their emotions more through gestures than words. For example, leaning towards things we like and avoiding things we dislike. According to a former Special Service agent, open palms facing up indicate a positive connection. Leaning away suggests building a barrier. Crossing the arms or legs is another gesture to pay attention to them. This behavior indicates defensiveness, anger, or self-protection if you see

anybody doing it. It can also signal discomfort or a desire to create a physical barrier between oneself and others. In some cases, it may simply be a comfortable position, so it's important to consider the context and other accompanying gestures when interpreting this body language.

If someone is learning and you say something that causes them to suddenly cross their arms, you may be sure that what you said upset them. Conversely, covering one's hands implies that person is hiding something, indicating that they are trying to calm themselves in an uncomfortable situation or under pressure. I'm not saying that body language is always a reliable indicator of someone's emotions, but it can certainly provide valuable insight into how a person is feeling. It's important to pay attention to these nonverbal cues in order to understand and communicate with others. Whether it's a subtle shift in posture or a more obvious gesture, body language can often speak louder than words.

TRICK TO STUDY PEOPLE 4

TRY TO INTERPRETE FACIAL EXPRESSION

Unless you've mastered the art of the poker face, your emotions will likely show on your face. Facial expressions can convey various emotions:

Deep frowns may signal anxiety or over thinking.

Genuine laughter is often marked by crow's feet, the grin lines of joy.

Pursed lips may indicate resentment, hatred, or fury, while tension can be displayed through a clenched mouth and grinding teeth. These are classified as smiles. It's fascinating to consider how our facial expressions can be windows into our emotions, conveying a rich tapestry of feelings without a single word spoken. Whether we realize it or not, our faces often reveal our innermost thoughts and sentiments to the world around us.

Reward smile: Raised eyebrows, lips drawn straight upward, and mouth dimples at the sides. This conveys compliments.

29

An affinitive grin has the lips pressed together and little dimples formed at the corners of the mouth. A token of affection and friendship.

The characteristics of a dominant grin include a lifted upper lip, pushed cheeks upward, wrinkled nose, deepened mouth-snap indentation, and elevated upper lids. A submissive grin is characterized by a closed mouth, slightly lowered head, and eyes looking upward. It is a sign of humility and respect.

A fake smile involves the lips being stretched tightly across the face, with little to no movement in the eyes. This can indicate insincerity or discomfort.

A polite smile is a simple upturn of the lips, often used in social situations as a sign of courtesy and acknowledgement.

TRICKS TO STUDY PEOPLE 5

DON'T RUN AWAY FROM TALK

Maybe you feel uneasy with small talk. However, it can be an opportunity to connect with the other person.

Participating in small talk lets you observe how someone behaves in regular situations. This way, you can easily spot any unusual behavior by comparing it to their usual demeanor .Small talk also helps to establish rapport and build trust with others. It creates a relaxed and friendly atmosphere, making it easier to transition into more meaningful conversations. So, even if it feels awkward at first, embracing small talk can lead to stronger connections and more fulfilling interactions.

CHAPTER THREE

TRICK TO STUDY PEOPLE 6

SCAN THE PERSON OVERAL BEHAVIOUR

At times, we may interpret someone's unease or worry based on specific actions, like looking down at the floor

HOW TO READ PEOPLE'S MIND

during a conversation. Yet, if you are familiar enough with them to recognize when they glance at the floor, you can discern whether they are simply relaxing or avoiding eye contact. Certain individuals have unique behaviors and tendencies, some of which "may just be mannerisms." Therefore, establishing a baseline of typical behavior in others will be advantageous. Developing the ability to notice any deviation from an individual's usual behavior is key. If you detect a change in their tone, pace, or body language, you will sense that something is amiss. Understanding these subtleties requires patience and observation. It's essential to avoid jumping to conclusions, as these deviations may not always indicate distress. At times, a change in behavior could simply reflect a shift in mood or circumstances. By remaining attentive and open-minded, we can better support those around us and offer assistance when needed.

TRICKS TO STUDY PEOPLE 7

ASK DIRECT QUESTION TO GET STRAIGHT ANSWER

Please keep the following in mind when asking questions: it's important to avoid ambiguity if you want direct response. Always provide clear questions that require a specific answer.

It's important to ask clear and direct questions. if you want to receive a specific response. Also, it's essential to avoid interrupting someone, while they are answering your questions. Instead, observe their behavior and the way they talk to better understand their thought process. A useful tip to learn more about someone's decision-making process is to look for "action words" in their statements. For example, if your supervisor says that she has "decided to go with brand X," it suggests that she is not impulsive and has considered other options before making a decision. Action words can reveal a person's approach to problem-solving.

TRICK TO STUDY PEOPLE 8

NOTICE THE WORD AND TONE USED

Pay attention to the language people use when you converse with them. When someone says, "This is the

second time I've been promoted," they are indicating that they have been promoted before. What's your take? The individuals rely on others to enhance their self-image. They seek your approval to bolster their self-assurance. Also, be mindful of the tone utilized: The volume and inflection of our voice can convey a great deal about our emotions. Sound frequencies create vibrations. Notice how a person's tone affects you as you listen to them. Does their tone soothe you? Or is it grating, snappy, or harsh? As we engage in dialogue, it's crucial to observe the nuances in people's expressions and body language. When an individual remarks, "I've encountered this issue previously," they are subtly indicating their familiarity with the situation. It's evident that they are seeking acknowledgment and validation, perhaps to affirm their competence.

CHAPTER FOUR

TRICK TO STUDY PEOPLE 9

PAY ATTENTION TO FLASHES OF INSIGHT

Furthermore, it's essential to remain attentive to the intonation and cadence employed in communication. The rhythm and pitch of one's speech can convey a spectrum of emotions. The resonance of a person's voice can have a calming effect or, conversely, provoke tension or unease. These subtleties play a significant role in shaping our interactions and perceptions.

CONCLUSION

Having the ability to read people is an extremely valuable skill, that can increase your awareness of the needs and challenges of those around you. This talent can also improve your EQ. The good news is that every individual has the capacity to read people, including you. The fact is, all you need to do is learn what to look for.